KYŌZAKURA

THE TREE THAT NEVER BLOSSOMED

SURBHI PANDEY

To all my precious readers, thankyou.

Contents

Acknowledgements   *xvii*

Preface   *xix*

Foreword   *xxi*

A playlist for the pages and your soul   *xxiii*

Prologue   *xxxi*

1. CHAPTER 1 - JUDE'S PERSPECTIVE   1

Part 1

Part 2

Part 3

Part 4

2. CHAPTER 2 - JUDE'S PERSPECTIVE   11

Part 5

Part 6

Part 7

Part 8

3. CHAPTER 3 - JUDE'S PERSPECTIVE   21

Part 9

Part 10

Part 11

Part 12

4. CHAPTER 4 - ZACH'S PERSPECTIVE   31

Part 13

Part 14

Part 15

5. CHAPTER 5 - ZACH'S PERSPECTIVE   39

Part 16

Part 17

Part 18

Contents

Part 19

    6. CHAPTER 6 - JUDE'S PERSPECTIVE   49

Part 20

Part 21

Part 22

Part 23

    7. CHAPTER 7 - JUDE'S PERSPECTIVE   59

Part 24

Part 25

Part 26

Part 27

    8. CHAPTER 8 - JUDE'S PERSPECTIVE   69

Part 28

Part 29

Part 30

Part 31

    9. CHAPTER 9 - JUDE'S PERSPECTIVE   79

Part 32

Part 33

Part 34

Part 35

    10. CHAPTER 10 - JUDE'S PERSPECTIVE   89

Part 36

Part 37

Part 38

Part 39

    11. CHAPTER 11 - ZACH'S PERSPECTIVE   99

Part 40

Contents

Part 41

Part 42

Part 43

12. CHAPTER 12 - JUDE'S PERSPECTIVE   109

Part 44

Part 45

Part 46

Part 47

13. CHAPTER 13 - JUDE'S PERSPECTIVE   119

Part 48

Part 49

Part 50

Part 51

14. CHAPTER 14 - JUDE'S PERSPECTIVE   129

Part 52

Part 53

Part 54

Part 55

15. CHAPTER 15 - JUDE'S PERSPECTIVE   139

Part 56

Part 57

Part 58

Part 59

Part 60

Part 61

16. CHAPTER 16 - JUDE'S PERSPECTIVE   153

Part 62

Part 63

Contents

Part 64

Part 65

Part 66

17. CHAPTER 17 - ZACH'S PERSPECTIVE   169

Part 67

Part 68

Part 69

Part 70

18. CHAPTER 18 - ZACH'S PERSPECTIVE   179

Part 71

Part 72

Part 73

Part 74

19. CHAPTER 19 - ZACH'S PERSPECTIVE   189

Part 75

Part 76

Part 77

Part 78

20. CHAPTER 20 - JUDE'S PERSPECTIVE   199

Part 79

Part 80

Part 81

Part 82

21. CHAPTER 21 - JUDE'S PERSPECTIVE   209

Part 83

Part 84

Part 85

Part 86

Contents

22. CHAPTER 22 - JUDE'S PERSPECTIVE 219

Part 87

Part 88

Part 89

Part 90

23. CHAPTER 23 - HEREY'S PERSPECTIVE 229

Part 91

Part 92

Part 93

Part 94

24. CHAPTER 24 - HEREY'S PERSPECTIVE 239

Part 95

Part 96

Part 97

Part 98

25. CHAPTER 25 - HEREY'S PERSPECTIVE 249

Part 99

Part 100

Part 101

Part 102

26. CHAPTER 26 - HEREY'S PERSPECTIVE 259

Part 103

Part 104

Part 105

Part 106

27. CHAPTER 27 - JUDE'S PERSPECTIVE 269

Part 107

Part 108

Contents

Part 109

Part 110

Part 111

28. CHAPTER 28 - HEREY'S PERSPECTIVE   281

Part 112

Part 113

Part 114

Part 115

29. CHAPTER 29 - HEREY'S PERSPECTIVE   291

Part 116

Part 117

Part 118

Part 119

30. CHAPTER 30 - JUDE'S PERSPECTIVE   301

Part 120

Part 121

Part 122

Part 123

31. CHAPTER 31 - JUDE'S PERSPECTIVE   311

Part 124

Part 125

Part 126

Part 127

32. CHAPTER 32 - JUDE'S PERSPECTIVE   321

Part 128

Part 129

Part 130

Part 131

Contents

33. CHAPTER 33 - JUDE'S PERSPECTIVE   331

Part 132

Part 133

Part 134

Part 135

34. CHAPTER 34 - JUDE'S PERSPECTIVE   341

Part 136

Part 137

Part 138

Part 139

Part 140

35. CHAPTER 35 - JUDE'S PERSPECTIVE   353

Part 141

Part 142

Part 143

Part 144

36. CHAPTER 36 - JUDE'S PERSPECTIVE   363

Part 145

Part 146

Part 147

Part 148

37. CHAPTER 37 - JUDE'S PERSPECTIVE   373

Part 149

Part 150

Part 151

Part 152

38. CHAPTER 38 - JUDE'S PERSPECTIVE   383

Part 153

Contents

Part 154

Part 155

Part 156

39. CHAPTER 39 - JUDE'S PERSPECTIVE   393

Part 157

Part 158

Part 159

Part 160

40. CHAPTER 40 - JUDE'S PERSPECTIVE   403

Part 161

Part 162

Part 163

Part 164

41. CHAPTER 41 - HEREY'S PERSPECTIVE   413

Part 165

Part 166

Part 167

Part 168

42. CHAPTER 42 - JUDE'S PERSPECTIVE   423

Part 169

Part 170

Part 171

Part 172

43. CHAPTER 43 - JUDE'S PERSPECTIVE   433

Part 173

Part 174

Part 175

Part 176

Contents

44. CHAPTER 44 - HEREY'S PERSPECTIVE   443

Part 177

Part 178

Part 179

Part 180

45. CHAPTER 45 - HEREY'S PERSPECTIVE   453

Part 181

Part 182

Part 183

Part 184

46. CHAPTER 46 - JUDE'S PERSPECTIVE   463

Part 185

Part 186

Part 187

Part 188

Part 189

47. CHAPTER 47 - JUDE'S PERSPECTIVE   475

Part 190

Part 191

Part 192

Part 193

48. CHAPTER 48 - JUDE'S PERSPECTIVE   485

Part 194

Part 195

Part 196

Part 197

49. CHAPTER 49 - JUDE'S PERSPECTIVE   495

Part 198

Contents

Part 199

Part 200

Part 201

   50. CHAPTER 50 - JUDE'S PERSPECTIVE   505

Part 202

Part 203

Part 204

Part 205

KYōZAKURA

The Tree

That

Never Blossomed

SURBHI PANDEY

Acknowledgements

I am so grateful that you kept faith in me mom and dad. And the biggest thankyou and all the credits to my brother. Thankyou to all these people who saw even a titbit of talent, a titbit of the potential that I might have in me. I wish I could garland you with my love. I love you all.

Preface

I didn't set out to write a book. I set out to survive moments that didn't have words until they did. This book is my attempt to hold what couldn't stay: emotions, people, pieces of myself. These poems were written in silence, in storm, in healing.

Each poem in here carries my heart, and I offer them to you not as polished art, but as raw reflections. If you find even one line that feels like home, then this book has done what it came to do.

Foreword

Poetry has always been a way for me to capture the moments between breaths—the fleeting thoughts, the unsaid words, the silence that carries meaning. Kyōzakura is a collection born from such moments. It is an exploration of beauty, pain, and everything that lies in between. The title itself—Kyōzakura, meaning "cherry blossoms in their fleeting beauty"—reminds me of how life, like the blossoms, is short but unforgettable. These poems were written in quiet corners and loud storms, each one a snapshot of emotions I couldn't always voice aloud.

This book isn't about perfect verse or polished lines. It is a piece of my soul that I have bared for you, the reader, to experience. I hope you find fragments of yourself within these words, and that, like cherry blossoms, they leave an impression even after they are gone.

Thank you for walking with me through these pages.

— Surbhi

A Playlist For The Pages And Your Soul

Sparks [by coldplay]

Can't help falling in love [by Elvis Presley]

Those eyes [by New West]

Open arms [by SZA and Travis scott]

My heart is buried in venice [by Ricky Montgomery]

Mr. loverman [by Ricky Montgomery]

Francis forever [by Mitski]

Line without a hook [by Ricky Montgomery]

Blue [by Yung kai]

I think they call this love [by Elliot James Reay]

You and I [by Diego Gonzalez]

Wildflower [by Yung kai]

Pause [by Prateek kuhad]

Yellow paper daisy [by When chai met toast]

The night we met [by Lord hurron]

Moral of the story [by Ashe]

Just say the words [by Matthew Ifield]

Here with me [by d4vd]

Use somebody [by Kings of leon]

You found me [by The fray]

Dark red [by Steve lacy]

Infrunamy [by Steve lacy]

Something about you [by Eyedress and Dent May]

I love you so [by The walters]

Lovers Rock [by TV girl]

Young [by Vacations]

Moonlight on the river [by Mac DeMarco]

Romantic Homicide [by d4vd]

Cloud nine [by Beach bunny]

Atlantis [by Seafret]

Car's outside [by James Arthur]

You're so vain [by Carly Simon]
Cold/mess [by Prateek Kuhad]

Bonne Lecture

May these words reach you gently, like cherry blossoms drifting on a spring breeze.

Prologue

This book that you're about to read is quite different from the books you must be reading. It is a set of poetry with each poem aligned in such a way that collectively, they somehow tell a story. A poem is supposed to put into words what your heart is feeling. In this book that you're about to read, each poem tells you about a part of the main lead's life, oh, who I totally forgot to introduce to you. So, here are the people you're about to meet as you dive deep into this book – There's Jude [The main lead], she's damn strong and so resilient . Then further in the book, you'll be meeting Zach, and then you'll meet Herey. All of them are interesting characters in themselves. You'll get to read poems all linked to each other in one way or the other, from all of their individual perspectives .

Enough of the introduction now, go grab your favourite drink and play your favourite music and let's get reading.

PROLOGUE

1. CHAPTER 1 - JUDE'S PERSPECTIVE

Miss Jude shuns all misery,

remorse this remorse that, oh none in her treasury.

And if she's never let nobody scar her heart,

what remorse, what haunting on her chart.

She is art, she is pure bliss,

no distress oh no sign of abyss.

She's the wild free stream in the woods you see,

she's the North sea.

No care of the unseen, oh not a single frown line,

all she knows is how to live, and how to shine.

She loves being, she loves the voyage,

no matter the waves, oh she's always geared up with the sails.

Not a single bone of loathe is within her,

resentment? Oh all of that's all blur.

She lives, oh all she knows is to live,

yes, to live, and not just strive.

2. CHAPTER 2 - JUDE'S PERSPECTIVE

The world I know is a beautiful place,

I love what's within me, I love me all parts,

hate or cheat, oh there's no trace

all around all unmatched hearts.

All around all I see,

all I see are radiant hearts, hearts like the alluring autumn's breeze.

Streets like a blank canvas with so many colours to paint,

and all skepticism is just to taint.

With all at peace with all at ease,

with no despair, all untainted hearts all clear seas,

and so I sometimes wonder if it can be,

oh the red string theory, will I ever see.

My heart beats loud for all this love,

for people in love for all hearty cov,

and just give out all love out that you can,

and people in love are people I stan.

3. CHAPTER 3 - JUDE'S PERSPECTIVE

Solitude's the home I desire

oh how I know that's my own empire,

oh what all I'll do to keep the stillness for eternity,

yes that and no uncertainty.

Question my sanity, oh you can't,

look at me and you won't,

I'll hug my heart I'll hug my soul,

all that for somebody else's love? Oh I'd never even crawl.

I am my peace, I am my tranquil,

I am the one who keeps that stupid flame strong, I'm the one who keeps it still,

how do I find peace in somebody's love?

When I am the love of my life and oh am I so enough.

I fear I'll find nobody,

my love ,oh who can embody,

well how can I dare to think I will,

that space in my heart oh nobody may fill.

4. CHAPTER 4 - ZACH'S PERSPECTIVE

You're as pretty as the sky in each phase,

or shall I say the cyclamen in the winter morning haze.

You're as serene as the water of swan,

or shall I say, the American guan.

You're what poets call divinity,

or shall I say Beethoven's 6th symphony.

You're like the moonlight hitting the water at siesta,

or shall I say the great Shakespeare's avesta.

You're as pretty as the unique,

you're as pretty as the euphoria which I may seek,

or the ballroom dance of   the epitome of elegance and skill,

or the spring which blooms the daffodil.

5. CHAPTER 5 - ZACH'S PERSPECTIVE

• 40 •

Oh Jude my Jude, I beg you please,

take all the vows, all promises, if that's what'll give you ease,

cannot you see how much I desire,

oh not for my desire, but please love me, I plea, oh it's just you I admire.

Deep within me, there's nothing of mine, nothing of that sort,

it's all you, oh it's all yours, oh how my love, how else do I court.

I pledge to you, oh my precious, I'll keep it safe,

oh without that love of yours I am a waif.

If you just love me, you will then see,

when love finds you it'll find you loved,

and if death finds me it'll find me alive,

yes it'll find me free.

And if what's inside of you, you just speak,

oh you'll save a soul from being wrecked,

and I hope death finds me just so alive,

and for me a happy death it does contrive.

6. CHAPTER 6 - JUDE'S PERSPECTIVE

I'm falling for you, I'm falling hard,

and to think why, would be just so absurd,

the girl who thought solitude was all hers, and to discard her grief she gave her all,

what may she say now that all her grief you stole.

Thought I'd never love you, oh how dumb was that,

and now I am whereat,

my heart and my mind are at a spat,

oh and for you my heart is an acrobat.

And I don't know how I will,

not love you oh for that I will have to kill,

pause that heart and kill my soul,

I'll have to bury myself whole.

Neither I know why I love you or how,

nor do I want to now.

All I know is you're now my muse,

why won't I love you, when I just can't refuse.

7. CHAPTER 7 - JUDE'S PERSPECTIVE

• 60 •

I'm trying, trying hard,

but how do I keep up my guard,

you hear me without me screaming,

You make it all a fairytale, like I'm dreaming.

But how do I keep up and not give up to you,

oh how is it that you just know, you just knew,

how do I not want you when you want me with no conditions,

how do I bring a halt to these inhibitions.

And when you show me how,

I'm all enough for you without me proving, without me having to vow,

and I want to love you straightaway,

oh just how for me you always allay.

I don't fear beginnings, but endings,

I'm scared of dreadful pretendings,

and if I was to love you love,

would you stay, mine of?

8. CHAPTER 8 - JUDE'S PERSPECTIVE

She was never the someone anyone loved,

never was she called beloved,

never loved right, she was always above'd,

"she's not worthy of love" someone always proved.

What she wanted was what she never got,

that ache in her heart, oh it always echoed,

She always looked at them being cradled,

"oh will that ever be me" she was wretchedly saddled.

She was never the one to light up the room,

she was never the yellow, all called her grey gloom.

Will she ever find the yellow, she wants to be,

racking her? But to what degree.

Lemons, oh there are a lot,

but how many sours before the sweet she got?

No alibi for life being so cruel,

is she always to be the fool?

9. CHAPTER 9 – JUDE'S PERSPECTIVE

Yearning, oh that's an understatement,

what's within me now is resentment,

never yet have I chanced upon what's called love,

and I sometimes sit and muse if or not I'm enough.

Craved for love, longed and longed,

but then upon me it has dawned,

I'll crave and die, oh I'll crave and die,

but alas will never stumble upon, will I?

And she who wears her heart out on her sleeves,

with love oh how each bond she weaves,

each time oh on love she grieves,

if she doesn't, love will find her who believes.

Will her yearning be heeded, oh ever be heeded,

will she ever find what's unsaid but needed,

and if love hounds her which I hope it does,

I hope she doesn't flee, I hope she doesn't hush.

10. CHAPTER 10 - JUDE'S PERSPECTIVE

Struggling, struggling to shun you,

well it sure is unyielding when you're slowly wiping that line I drew,

and well when I try to draw it back right there,

oh it's to waste you just declare.

And I'm trying not to fall in love,

but to not love you why is it such a task, all sentiment why do I shove?

And then I sit and ponder what's so wrong,

but then what's so right too, oh where do I belong?

To push you away, is what the mind wants to do,

but then I ask me what lapse did the heart do?

That fear is what's holding me,

molding heart but dread as big as the sea.

And how do I have the change of mind,

the change that'll make me leave all terror behind?

Oh you're wiping away the line I drew,

oh how, and how do I shun you.

11. CHAPTER 11 - ZACH'S PERSPECTIVE

Oh Jude, my Jude,

how don't you see?

Oh will I break your heart,

oh how can that be me .

Oh Jude my lovely Jude,

moment after moment I think,

how do I not love you,

for if it's not you who I love, who do I love,

oh I'd rather let my heart hit a berg and sink.

How do I tell you that I won't,

oh break your heart ? I hope I don't.

And if you think I will, [oh my Jude do you still?],

rip my heart into pieces and yours with joy you may fill.

And if you walk with me and not by me,

how will I keep in me all that ecstasy and all that glee,

to be the subject of your love, oh what an honor,

for within my heart you already reside and you're it's most delicate adorner.

12. CHAPTER 12 - JUDE'S PERSPECTIVE

There once was a tallow lamp,

with self - loathing oh she was damp.

Admirers you ask? Oh there were abundant,

but all she wanted was to be distant.

So much so, of her self - contempt,

she smoldered and smoldered to the utmost extent.

Burnt out, oh how dead she was,

she had counted in her thousands of flaws.

That one moth saw not a single flaw,

the dreamiest agony was the only thing he saw,

"you'll suffer, you won't remain", oh so warned she,

you think he listened? Oh did he?

He went to her, her smoldering flame hugged him tight,

so surrendered in love, neither did he resist, nor did he fight.

What do you think happened to both? We know, so let's just revamp,

there once was a dead tallow lamp,

once in time with oh so much of self - loathing she was damp.

13. CHAPTER 13 - JUDE'S PERSPECTIVE

Failed, yes, oh I failed,

my heart won, your name is nailed,

how was it feasible for me, for me to win,

oh I saw visions, prettier than the borealis, prettier than virtue, prettier than sin.

To give in, how would I have ceased mmy core,

oh I couldn't, I just could not anymore.

What else now is my core's desire,

you were its sole, and the sole it'll admire.

It now worships me, and why would it not,

the sole that it honored, it has now got.

A victory you are, a victory over my fear,

a win to me, which is so dear.

A victory that's today, a victory that'll be tomorrow,

a win to me, or a trophy you'd like to show ?

Well now that I've lost and then won,

I don't know if I will be burnt, now that I'm reaching for the sun.

14. CHAPTER 14 - JUDE'S PERSPECTIVE

Music to the ears,

a symphony to be heard,

how can you find a flaw,

that is just absurd.

A voice sweeter than the water of Lapland sea,

a voice which fills one's heart with everlasting ecstasy and glee.

Perpetual, oh so is my love for you,

with thee all my sorrow and agony flew.

Your melody tingles in me,

as Adonis's love ran through Aphrodite,

it runs through me every inch, every bit,

by your tune I am struck, I am hit.

Yet you seem to find a flaw in you,

when you're the greatest piece of music and the most alluring view.

Centuries and centuries, I know it is a cue,

I could have existed in any, but I had to with you.

15. CHAPTER 15 - JUDE'S PERSPECTIVE

Muse oh muse I love you so,

and I'll do all it takes for you to know,

just that I love you as I love the golden hour,

muse oh muse I love you as I love the golden summer's rainshower.

Oh muse my muse I hope you know,

just that whenever the world tells you to kneel and bow,

and when the splinters, they make your you bleed,

you'll find me open winged, yes you will indeed.

Arms outstretched I'll caress your soul,

and you'll nestle safe while we make your grief a parole.

While you rest your head on my perch I'll hold you tight,

and I'll embrace you, embrace you with all my might.

And so when you cry, cry in my arms,

cry until your grief smolders and my love outcharms.

Oh muse my lovely muse I'll tell you so,

you are now safe in my embrace I'll let you know.

And oh muse when I can't caress your soul ,

of mine part by part I'll give you dole by dole,

oh muse for you I'll rip out my heart and place it next to yours,

and then it'll do the same until all your agony it procures.

16. CHAPTER 16 - JUDE'S PERSPECTIVE

When I'm buried down there 6 feet or so,

with all the evocation that they'll never know,

the coup d'oeil still thriving in me,

the glimpses that they'll never see.

And when I'm buried down there 6 feet or so,

with bugs eating my brain,

they'll get the prettiest visions of what I know,

visions of moonlit stardust, of starlit white snow.

And so when I'm buried down there 6 feet or so,

with the grimmest of heart for you to know,

they'll see unimaginable bits of cosmos disbanding into the soil,

and won't move an inch without bumping into a bit of the memory coil.

And when it will be so that I'm buried under there 6 feet or so,

with a part of everything slowly fading into nothingness that'll never ever show,

the whorl of visions will slowly grow dim,

for a moment they'll be star - strudded, they'll be blanched,

as they'll see a whole world of stardust inside that bright white and pink receptacle of memories, a case.

And then the visions will grow dim and then dimmer,

as they then partake of the last bits of my brain that was once the source of   non- ending shimmer.

17. CHAPTER 17 - ZACH'S PERSPECTIVE

I'm losing it, losing your soul in me,

and now it's like I have to burst your bubble, end all your glee.

Oh it's arduous for me now, exhausting my soul,

never did I think for my love you'd have to bawl.

But it's like I'm caged,

each memory in me once held your tune,

your laugh, your smile, that once delighted me,

oh why now can I not bear to see.

And you once told me how,

how I speak your tongue and you won't have to translate your soul now,

oh how do I put all together?

Oh all I want is to end this "forever".

And you will say the I love you isn't the same,

and you'll someday see the smoldering flame,

oh well it's my desire for the someday to just be imminent,

what all can I do now, but for crushing your soul, repent.

18. CHAPTER 18 - ZACH'S PERSPECTIVE

All the love I had for you,

it's fading into nothingness, with you having no clue,

I no longer possess the grace to love you,

and the way you love me so profound, if only you knew.

And the way you speak, and the way that you giggle,

I just can't harbor the will to bloom in your light, how do I not diddle?

It wasn't my will crush your heart,

it wasn't my will to snap you out of that dream, to tear you apart.

You look at me with spark in your eyes,

oh how do I tell you, how do I tell more lies,

how do I tell you I'm losing all I had for you,

I'm losing the warmth, I'm losing the dew.

And I know I will soon,

soon lose your trust, I'll lose that tune.

And you'll lose your utmost yearning,

and your heart soon will be on fire, burning.

19. CHAPTER 19 - ZACH'S PERSPECTIVE

I am now done, done with all,

and I have no worry, whether you cry, whether you bawl.

And what was with you, it was all chaos,

anybody's, oh it'll be your loss.

Bear you? Oh I don't even wish I could,

and I have no more strength to do any of the "good".

So let us now both part our hearts,

only for good oh we're clearing our charts.

Leave my hand now, oh will you,

oh I'm sure you'll find your blue,

the blue I know you've always looked for,

I hope I knew you enough or......

And if I had your life in my hands,

I show you remorse for killing all of it, I hope it stands,

I contrite for killing all of you within me,

but what I had for you, oh I just couldn't see.

20. CHAPTER 20 - JUDE'S PERSPECTIVE

Left me grieving? Yes you did,

made my heart into sand, she shadowed and you hid,

an unaware fool is what you think of me,

well, what can I do but agree.

Yes how can I be "love" for someone, yes I can't,

when there are millions and millions who can enchant,

the tulip in between roses, the toad in between fishes,

never the worthy "love" someone misses.

So damn silly for me to even think,

how can I be somebody's "her" even for once, even just to think,

I thought I'd be loved, the greatest comic I could think of,

do I cry now? Or do I look at the mirror and laugh, and just laugh?

This is my moment, I thought with wonders,

you shattered my soul, drained my heart, you left me feeling like a blunder,

oh and you told me you loved me first, and you told me you loved me the most,

I thought the battle, the kingdom was mine, oh how have I lost?

21. CHAPTER 21 - JUDE'S PERSPECTIVE

• 210 •

Neither somebody's "I saw her today",

nor am I "she took away all my gray".

Neither somebody's "she made me smile",

nor am I "for her I'd walk a mile".

Never possibly the one who gives you peace,

or the one who makes your heart feel at ease.

I'll probably never be the one who comes to your mind when you feel contented,

rather the one you'd think of whenever you feel resented.

How do I make me a subject for love,

without crossing oceans and oceans to be worthy of?

I'm not the muse you'd fondly ponder about,

well never unconditional, I really doubt.

Always an option, never the choice,

always has had the unheard voice.

You've filled my head with words and made it a cask,

"and how's she so poetic" you ask?

22. CHAPTER 22 - JUDE'S PERSPECTIVE

Maybe I'm not your favourite muse anymore,

because I probably am not the girl I used to be before.

Maybe not too shy, maybe just a little more sly,

maybe not the muse who used to be an eccedentesiast just to cry.

I'm aware you still hope,

to bring me "back to life", but I already tied me with a rope,

I hung me in the forest of guilt for you to never see,

hung to death now, you'll never feel that glee.

How creeped was my soul,

for it to just ball up and crawl,

how's yours I'd love to ask,

you can now no more use the guilt mould to cast.

Maybe I'll be back, maybe I won't,

maybe I'll stain my cheeks with blood, oh I hope I don't.

Your favourite muse, blind is what I used to be,

just to be an alexithymic for all to see.

23. CHAPTER 23 - HEREY'S PERSPECTIVE

Hey don't you know so,

hey daylight don't you know?

Don't you now how exceedingly I am in love,

don't you know how for me you've been sent from the heavens above.

Ever since I've laid my eyes on you,

my heart's been on fire, oh is it a cue?

Oh your eyes like starfire have lit my soul,

that heart of mine oh darl you stole.

And you might not see in you what I see,

oh but trust me darl you're as ethereal as anybody can ever be,

oh Jude how do I tell you I love you more,

I love you more than the seapiper loves the shore.

And I've regretted joy and I've regretted love,

I've regretted having a soul and the emotion thereof,

but on you oh darl I'll even bet,

that falling for you, oh I have no regret.

24. CHAPTER 24 - HEREY'S PERSPECTIVE

Fool oh fool you'll never know,

what you reap is what you sow,

I hope you know who you fumbled,

with all that greed I know you will be humbled.

A day will come when you will know,

how she is a gem and oh I vow,

I'll love her so profound I'll make you wonder,

I'll make you regret your dumb blunder.

How were you such a fool to leave her behind,

somebody with her demeanor? Someone you'll never find,

and oh to not see her worth you were so blind,

she is Aphrodite redefined.

She's gorgeous, she's kind, the epitome of grace,

I'll love her soul, her heart I'll embrace,

oh what you'll reap is what you'll sow,

and that, you're a fool who'll never know.

25. CHAPTER 25 - HEREY'S PERSPECTIVE

If I come to you, and if I take your hand,

and with my heart in my hand afront you I stand,

and if I tell you how you're etched into my heart,

will you give me yours, just a part?

Will I be the subject of your love?

Or will I be disillusioned, oh I dream of,

I dream of what's right infront of me,

oh how much I adore you, will you see?

And if I come to you and say,

and I take your hands if I may,

I'm yours all yours, oh there's no daze,

oh with an "indeed" my heart will you amaze?

Or will I be disheartened, left in the cold,

and if I am left hanging for tales to be told,

an act of love will I regret,

or what I desire I will get?

26. CHAPTER 26 - HEREY'S PERSPECTIVE

She's that one dew drop in the icy winter mornings,

that smile of hers is fairer than all adornings,

oh and how she wears her charm,

enough to just rip my heart out, how do I be so calm.

Her eyes like pearls adorn her face,

oh just how they shine in such grace.

Oh how she just squints them as she chuckles,

oh my oh my I could drown in those crinkles.

Her hair oh it's like a stream of gold,

oh and like waves in the ocean when rolled,

oh and if she was to strangle me I would,

I would die a death of such peace if I could.

Her face it shines, shines as she's walking sun,

and I won't be so silly to call her the moon,

oh and such is her glow, the moon faces plight,

oh her charm, her radiance, blinded, I'd lose my sight.

27. CHAPTER 27 - JUDE'S PERSPECTIVE

I went to the coffee shop down the street,

that has seen plenty of hearts meet.

The air in the room, always filled with love,

as if it was made for heartmates above.

The coffee still tastes alike,

the smell of it still gives my heartbeat a spike.

I felt the same warmth as last winters,

that one chair still gives me a warm hug though to my heart it feels like thousands of splinters

A lot of giggles, a lot of shy smiles,

which are now as distant as miles and miles,

while all has changed, all has not,

reminiscent of the warm smile I had last november sitting in the same spot.

I still go there in hopes of getting a glimpse,

in hopes that it's not just me yearning and pining ever since,

to feel that comforting presence just once more,

but alas return with the same yearning I had before.

I dashed when I saw my favourite spot slowly drifting,

heart throbbing, eyes sobbing and no hopes lifting.

But fear paralyzed me as it moved farther and farther away,

and then, I realized my favourite spot was never mine to say.

28. CHAPTER 28 - HEREY'S PERSPECTIVE

I walked up to you, I held your hand,

standing in front of you with a promise band,

and if you pardon then I may,

show you my love and this is what I would say.

You walked in like cool summer breeze,

oh all that glamour you made me freeze,

eyes like stars, your smile's like the fourth moon,

voice like somebody playing the flute's sweetest tune.

Looked into your eyes I saw a spark,

a spark that can light up hundreds of rooms dark,

I wonder if I can love you right,

oh love say yes I'll love you, love you with all my might.

Sun hit my face with the morning blaze,

I got up in the prettiest haze,

something that gave me such joy extreme,

oh doomed am I how can it be a dream.

29. CHAPTER 29 - HEREY'S PERSPECTIVE

I went to you, oh I finally did,

told you all and all I've ever hid,

told you how your stroke makes me shiver,

oh how a single glance makes me quiver.

Your heart fails thousands of the purest of diamonds,

the softest of silk oh are failed by your hands,

the prettiest angel I know, oh you define perfection,

the cherry blossom darling is a quarter of your reflection.

I'll give you the world and beyond it if you ask,

oh baby in my affection I'll let you bask,

you deserve all the warmth and I'll let you know therefore,

for your love darling I'll even implore.

I'll bring the world at your feet,

just love me love and I'll never cheat.

Your heart and soul baby I promise I will caress,

Oh darling if you just say yes.

30. CHAPTER 30 - JUDE'S PERSPECTIVE

I'm scared of love, oh not the idea of it,

I'm scared of my love remaining unrequited yes I admit.

And I'm scared of falling that way again,

I'm scared my bones will wane in that same rain.

I'm scared as I know I'm subpar,

I'm scared as I know I'll always scar.

I'm scared for that thing in my chest,

I'm scared, I'm oh so scared to nest.

And I'm so petrified that I might,

go into deep dark woods at night,

and I'll unleash that thing out of my chest and lock it up,

I'll lock it in a diamond cage and then never let it rup.

And how do I eradicate this fear,

I'm terrified it might never leave now that it does steer,

and it's my desire it never leaves and always steers,

or you will come greet me next on the biers.

31. CHAPTER 31 - JUDE'S PERSPECTIVE

What have I done to deserve all the unfair,

to even ask now? Oh I do not dare.

Maybe it's all me, maybe it's all my fault,

maybe it's within me, or maybe it's all by cause of my exalt.

Why so cruel, why always me,

when will this end? When will I be set free?

Hurt me leave me bruise me to the core,

all faith's now corpsed, oh nobody can restore.

Why is it always reasons to leave and never to stay,

all that sentiment, why is it always display?

Well what else may I expect,

it's my own heart that I always fail to protect.

How do I fight with life itself,

eyes all dead since I was twelve,

I've lost myself to all the worst,

a lot to blame but I first.

32. CHAPTER 32 - JUDE'S PERSPECTIVE

My prayers are lost voices,

and so I've learnt to live with the past, to live with my choices,

and I've given up wishing on my plea to be heard,

wishing and hoping, just so absurd.

All lights lost, all love lost,

learnt so many lessons, but at what cost.

And I begged to be heard just one more time,

trusting somebody, oh is it a crime.

Now I bleed tears of agony,

and in my heart I've lost all symphony,

begged on my knees to get what I want,

all those reflections oh now haunt.

Now I live and do not think,

what was to be lost is lost, I just let it sink,

well now cutting muself to fit the cube, oh how would that help,

to give up on all? Oh I'm just on the brink.

33. CHAPTER 33 - JUDE'S PERSPECTIVE

Yes I hid it within me,

I hid it for nobody to see,

I hid it for you to not see, but I just cannot seem to forget,

what he did with my heart how he tore it apart and I let.

And to forgive my soul I will,

I will do what he did to my heart,

I'll make you take the red pill, I'll crush you into bits,

and then I'll take a part and put it in the hole in my chest where it fits.

It was unfair to me and so it will be to you,

I'll be shattering you and you'll have no cue.

He wrecked my heart and I'll wreck yours,

and I'll make sure your heart softens and pours.

It'll be a "love" story to be remembered,

one in which a loving heart becomes decembered,

a love story with pure agony, hate, and no love,

lover, oh and pain thereof.

34. CHAPTER 34 - JUDE'S PERSPECTIVE

Oh should I, should I give you a shot,

well to lose now, what have I even got.

To keep me sane, yes what do I need,

yes I do still fear, yes, indeed.

Oh well all that heart how do I have no heart,

and if I once more get torn apart,

oh just vow to me that you will caress,

with all that heart in you, how may I not say yes?

HEREY'S PERSPECTIVE

That one wish I had in me,

oh love now that you have granted,

how do I tell you what is occurring within me,

you have presented me with the one thing I've wanted.

Hey my Jude, I'll give you the galaxy,

though it my sound like a fallacy,

you're entitled to all the rays of sunshine,

oh I'll give you the galaxy, now that you're mine.

35. CHAPTER 35 - JUDE'S PERSPECTIVE

Yes I once was so alive,

yes I once was so naive,

the eyes that now seem dead and done,

yes they once shone prettier than the sun.

Cold I might be for you to judge,

when I'm tired, oh how'd someone make that lively heart trudge.

Oh how do I tell it to beat again,

when I failed to save it, when such a fool I had been.

"Love"? To me that's a foreign term,

"love for me", strange, who can ever affirm.

That strange fear gripped me once,

should've gripped me tight, should've gripped me to death, should've ended me once and
for all.

The lips that now speak poison ivy,

spoke once the sweetest of that bean pie navy,

and if there ever was an ocean of guilt I would dive,

yes I once was so alive.

36. CHAPTER 36 - JUDE'S PERSPECTIVE

You praise love, you worship it,

you worship it, you cherish it every bit.

And you're Pheidias if love's Athena,

and you're the white dove if love's selena.

And for you I am life,

and you say "what better religion than life?"

You're teaching me how it feels,

how it feels to be seen without performing oh and that conceals.

Thy love is a calm breeze,

and how is it so frenzied all at once, oh cease,

I'll never want to know why so,

because not loving is your greatest woe.

And you make me want to be all yours,

and I want to tell you all that secures,

oh how your affection conceals , oh how it heals,

and for this, afront you the whole world bows and kneels.

37. CHAPTER 37 - JUDE'S PERSPECTIVE

• 374 •

I look at you, look at you and wonder,

what have you done to deserve any of this, this blunder,

of all of my choices, will this be the worst,

I ponder and ponder on what was with me first.

Oh why are you to be faulted, why are you to be blamed,

and when you have done not a thing to be framed,

I think on what all I have thought of,

and I think of how you with no voracity you love.

I've kept in me yes all that rage,

and I've locked my heart up in a cage,

but then anew I think of you,

of all that you've done, of all that you do.

Oh how you call me precious,

how can I be so cruel, oh so vicious,

and I have thought , thought of not,

not handing you my heart but you have already got.

38. CHAPTER 38 - JUDE'S PERSPECTIVE

And if I break your heart and soul too,

and do all that I wanted to,

and if I embitter you, so you resent me,

will I forget all, will I really be free?

And if I break your heart and your sentiment I hurt,

will I ever forgive me, will I let go, will it ever go away, that dirt?

I'll bruise you and then if I don't say a word,

will I be pardoned, released, will I still be heard?

They say your chest remembers all that is heard,

and if I wound, mine still hasn't buried any word, each word.

And when I know how it is to drown,

how do I push you into the waters, wouldn't the benevolent in me frown?

I was drenched, drowned in the rain,

storms and storms, why would I let you sail through that pain.

And if I'm as bitter as the world was to me,

there wouldn't be much of a separation between us, would there be?

39. CHAPTER 39 - JUDE'S PERSPECTIVE

How do I break your heart oh dear,

how do I tell you that now I fear,

fear of losing my soul oh that's you,

oh I've been a deceiver and you have no clue.

I can't lose you, oh I cannot, not for billions,

and cause my love for you, that's in trillions,

darl I was a fool, darl how could I,

how could I envision causing you pain, I'd rather die.

You've shown me love,

you've proved me love, I found my lost home in you, the moon to my dove.

And oh how you have that likewise fear in you,

a fear of losing me, darl for me that's so new.

You've put my heart at ease,

and stay this way for eternity will you please,

and if I wound your heart, dear mine'll ache too,

and that's the last thing I'd do.

40. CHAPTER 40 - JUDE'S PERSPECTIVE

Thought I'll never again be in love,

all those damn feelings in a huge chest I'd shove.

Thought I'll be composed and blase',

oh but with you how may that be the case.

You loved me when I was aloof,

gave me your all when I showed reproof,

how will my love ever be enough,

how will I ever repay you, love.

I'm falling for you when I thought I wouldn't,

and I won't repel, should I or shouldn't,

and if falling for you means a heartbreak,

oh dear you're worth putting my life at stake.

I'll fall for you, I'll break my bones,

I'll tell you all and all in whispered tones,

thought all those feelings I'd shove,

now how is it so that I am in love.

41. CHAPTER 41 - HEREY'S PERSPECTIVE

To love you? Oh you think I'm a fool,

for you my love I'm a nightmare, worse than a ghoul,

I'll break you darl to such extent,

so dire you will be, you won't even resent.

Why do I give somebody what I have always craved for?

It's always sorrow that I've worn,

and that who has ever held me without me falling apart,

and that who has ever held me without crushing my heart.

And that you think I'll love you, great for you to think,

how will I when somebody taught my heart to hate, somebody made my heart shrink.

And you find your home nestled in my arms,

well how would you even know it's the start of storms.

And I'll kill the core within you like mine once was killed,

oh when my own heart was the victim, somebody the culprit, and the fear instilled.

And I'll do all that was done to me,

and just for once I won't be the broken one, this I guarantee.

42. CHAPTER 42 - JUDE'S PERSPECTIVE

How is it now, how can somebody love me,

I'm terrified of how my joy may flee,

I thought I was a being not to be loved,

and now how have I found you to love me oh darl, oh my beloved.

I'm yours, all yours,

with you I may peruse all possible vows,

and darl, hand in hand we'll mold a heart,

one that has a part of mine and of yours a part.

And I'll love you like loving you is breathing,

like if I don't my heart may stop beating,

yes I'll love you like there's no tomorrow,

and I'll love you so all your grief I can borrow.

You call me darl don't you in the prettiest way,

and why does my own name now feel stray,

oh love I'll keep you hidden, all mine,

oh for me this once how did the stars align.

43. CHAPTER 43 - JUDE'S PERSPECTIVE

I've never seen the "pretty" in me,

or the kind of kind you see.

All I've seen in me is peak poetry,

which brings thee great ecstasy.

Confused you say? Oh yes I am,

it ain't an everlasting tune to jam.

"pretty" you say? It's just a myth,

equivalent to the love for which I breathe.

Despite all, heaven is somebody's eyes,

somebody's smile that's prettier than the northern skies.

Maybe "pretty" is a pretty myth,

but pretty is for you to exist with.

Pretty is that you exist,

you're the peaks and I'm all over you as mist.

And yet you see the "pretty" in me,

which I'm too much of a fool to see.

44. CHAPTER 44 - HEREY'S PERSPECTIVE

And if I hurt you, and if you resent me,

and you will hate me but to what degree,

the exasperation in you will rise,

and for you I'll paint all skies, grey skies.

And you think it's us against the whole world,

how hurt will you be when all is unfurled?

And you show emotion thinking I might,

thinking I might love you but I hate you for all things right.

You love me so loud,

so loud but I am deaf,

and you love me like love's what you breathe,

but I love the dead.

Oh when you say sorry, for all that you do,

and then I tell you how I love you,

and I know you will be so so wronged,

and I'll get all the euphoria that I have longed.

45. CHAPTER 45 - HEREY'S PERSPECTIVE

How she left when I needed her utmost,

in her heart you ask? She was never a host.

Broke me to the greatest extent,

told all she was the one, oh who to I vent?

Loved her when she needed utmost,

turns out, yes I did overhost,

I'll never be the same, yes I know I won't,

let somebody break me? I hope I don't.

I'll break them first, I know I will,

you say my joy somebody will steal?

I'll steal their peace and hand them grief,

oh now that I am not so naive.

She tore tore me apart and I'll tear you down,

hope you don't hate me hope you don't frown,

what she did with me I'll hope you feel,

I'll break you in ways to take you back affront God you'll kneel.

46. CHAPTER 46 - JUDE'S PERSPECTIVE

I could drown in the gloss of them,

they're scintillating, as I recall the brightest of the brown gem.

The gloss of those indiscernible eyes,

eyes that are as indecipherable as the night skies.

The crescent shaped ruby inside of my skull,

that has now become dejected and dull,

has yet treasured the glory of those brown jaspers ,

the tales of which are heard by I in whispers.

I feel the exasperation ascending within me,

and I beg to them and I plea,

as they belittle the glamour of those celestial masterpieces,

and how the preturbation within I ceases,

as thy grandeur captivates me through thee eyes,

the splendor for which I might or might not suffice.

It will for eternity remain undiscovered,

on how sie got so incandescent uncovered,

when those two bits of the cluster stared into her two bits to entrust her.

And there was the sparkle in her eyes one time before,

the jaspers lost their charm and all of it tore.

47. CHAPTER 47 - JUDE'S PERSPECTIVE

I am the unluckiest of all,

yes the worst, the unlucky soul,

the corpse with no one by her side,

with the chest of misery open wide.

And if only I was loved right ,

if only there was not one sleepless night,

but who's so fortuned to have such fate,

well not me I know, I can never sate.

And you ask me what love is,

love is what I have none and what I'll always miss.

Such fate you've given me oh divine,

oh for me why do the stars never align?

I have nobody and I'll have nobody,

in the end nobody's heart is a soddy,

therefore how may I fantasize being in one,

well when I know for me the sun never shone.

48. CHAPTER 48 - JUDE'S PERSPECTIVE

Isn't it rousing,

within your heart mustn't it be carousing,

to be treasured by a lovestruck wordsmith,

that shapes each bond into words as fine as a goldsmith would do to a gold sheet.

The litterateur who tends to be forlorn,

despondent's what she tends to be,

by cause of what the words pour out though torn,

loves through words that add to her beauty as a rose to a thorn.

You're always in my head though in a disguise,

and you'll probably never die in my eyes.

Though I might be like a guitar with no one to strum,

you'll never feel unloved when my heart is your home,

cause darling I'm the poet and you're the poem.

49. CHAPTER 49 - JUDE'S PERSPECTIVE

Glued to the shadowed ground I am,

oh startled I was, by that wham,

just when I thought harmony reigned,

all of it milled me, left me all stained.

And how much more, how much more will I hurt?

Will I through every turn take up the dirt?

Am I so unworthy, so much so to again and again be thrown,

to be once praised and then never again be worn.

Oh I won't let it, how can I,

to be the victim, to end up crushed, just to cry,

oh that heart of mine that is so tender,

afront the vile how can I surrender.

No, I'll pick it up,

and as long as I have me that life in me won't ever stop,

I'll pick me up, keep me safe and sound,

so sheltered I will be that no person can ever hound.

50. CHAPTER 50 - JUDE'S PERSPECTIVE

There once was a queen, who had forsaken the glow of her worth,

it was dimmed by the world's hush, dead, buried deep in earth.

So unremembered was her virtue, value smoldering all so dusty,

all too dead, all had gotten so rusty.

She was the one to dance on each tune each note,

a sunflower she was, so gleeful she was, she'd float.

Oh the heart she had, the purest of diamonds would falter,

oh Jude, oh love how breezy you were, oh how you'd balter .

Oh Jude why do you seek love out and around,

oh love, oh my Jude you are now found,

and oh adored, I hope you now see the light,

oh my precious, you ARE love personified.

And besides my treasured, you've for forever been all that you've pursued,

oh and you would question God on why he would always preclude,

oh my cherished, you've always been the moon you've been chasing, oh dove,

after all anguish my love, halt your quest, the veil is now off, YOU are love.

"Everything that you love will probably be lost, but in the end, love will return in another way"

- Franz Kafka